Easy FLORAL Appliqué
PATTERNS

Eula Mae Long

American Quilter's Society
P. O. Box 3290 • Paducah, KY 42002-3290
www.AQSquilt.com

Located in Paducah, Kentucky, the American Quilter's Society (AQS) is dedicated to promoting the accomplishments of today's quilters. Through its publications and events, AQS strives to honor today's quiltmakers and their work and to inspire future creativity and innovation in quiltmaking.

EDITOR: BARBARA SMITH
GRAPHIC DESIGN: ELAINE WILSON
COVER DESIGN: MICHAEL BUCKINGHAM
PHOTOGRAPHY: CHARLES R. LYNCH

Library of Congress Cataloging-in-Publication Data

Long, Eula Mae.
    Easy floral appliqué patterns / By Eula Mae Long.
        p.cm.
    ISBN 1-57432-831-X
    1.   Appliqué--Patterns.   2.   Patchwork--Patterns.   3.   Quilting.   4
Flowers in art.   I. Title.

    TT779.L65 2003
    746.46'041--dc22
                            2003021335

Additional copies of this book may be ordered from the American Quilter's Society, PO Box 3290, Paducah, KY 42002-3290; 800-626-5420 (orders only please); or online at www.AQSquilt.com. For all other inquiries, call 270-898-7903.

Dedication

I dedicate this book to the memory of my late mother, Nellie M. Green James, who was an excellent seamstress and must have had an abundance of patience to teach me to sew.

VICTORIAN ROSE, 80" x 100". Bed quilt, pieced by the author and hand quilted by Edna Buhler, Salem, Oregon. Block pattern on page 78.

Acknowledgments

I'd like to thank a special group of friends, the Capitol Quilters of Salem, Oregon, for their encouragement and many useful suggestions.

Thanks also go to...

Edna Buhler for hand quilting;

Marie Warden for machine quilting;

and

The American Quilter's Society, for giving me the opportunity to share my appliqué designs with other quilters.

Contents

Introduction

This book is dedicated to the members of my quilt group, but truly, I have to say the inspiration came from some women I talked to at a quilt show in Wichita, Kansas. I had tired feet, so I sat down to rest, and it wasn't long until about six other quilters were resting, too. We began discussing our favorite subject ... appliqué. There were few appliqué quilts in this beautiful show, which started the women talking about what types of designs they liked to sew. They didn't want folk art patterns or the beautiful Baltimore-type appliqué, which had so many little pieces to handle. What they wanted were more modern designs, especially flowers, with large pieces that were easy to see and easy to handle. A quilt teacher in the group said she believed that beginning and intermediate appliquérs had few designs to choose from, especially if they lived in small towns.

I went home to Nebraska, where I lived at that time, and I dwelled on this problem and realized how true those women's words were. We needed more designs that would appeal to the average appliquér. So my job of designing began. Since my love of flowers comes close to my love of appliqué, the job was more joy than work, especially because I've been designing most of my own appliqué quilts for some time.

So enjoy, and may your days be filled with appliqué.

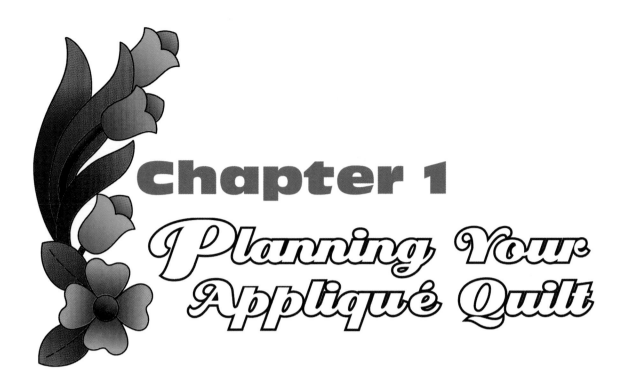

Chapter 1
Planning Your Appliqué Quilt

Selecting Your Blocks

Once you have looked over the photographs and patterns, you have some decisions to make before you make a mad rush to a fabric shop or start digging through your many boxes of scraps.

What block or blocks have you decided to use for your project? You can choose one block and repeat it to make a whole quilt or choose several designs to make a modern sampler quilt. Another option is to make a large central design, such as a large basket of flowers, and select blocks to go around it, medallion-style.

Whatever you choose, make a sample of each of your chosen blocks before you go any further with the whole project. A sample block will give you a better idea of what colors you do and don't want in your project. Be sure to balance the color in your appliqué pieces. For example, if you put a yellow flower on one side of the basket, try to have a yellow flower on the opposite side. In addition, you can change the shapes of the leaves or reposition them. You can change the flowers, too, and why not? It's your project. You can also change the size of the patterns if you want a larger or smaller block. A good photocopy machine will do the job.

Setting Your Blocks

How are you going to put your blocks together? Look over the diagrams on page 8 for ideas. Blocks can be set block to block, alternated with plain blocks, sewn together with setting strips, or set in many more ways.

If you are making a bed quilt, you have a variety of settings to choose from. In some of the settings, there is room for a large central design. A pattern is included in the pullout section for a large basket of flowers that makes a pretty quilt center. Patterns are also given for

FIG. 1. Blocks set side by side

FIG. 3. Blocks set with sashing strips

FIG. 4. Blocks set with corner triangles and sashing

FIG. 2. Appliqué blocks set with alternate plain blocks

appliqué border designs on pages 74–75. To help you plan your bed-sized quilt, refer to the Quilt Sizes chart on page 9. You can choose borders in widths and colors to complete the size you need and the look you want for your quilt.

For an on-point setting, use the Diagonal Sets table on page 10 to help you figure out how many blocks you will need. For example, a 14" block set on point is approximately 20" across, from corner to corner.

On-point blocks require setting triangles for the sides and corners of the quilt. To create the side triangles, cut a fabric square that is at least 1¼" larger than your block's diagonal measurement. Cut the square diagonally twice to yield four side triangles. For the corner triangles, cut a fabric square that is at least ⅞" larger than half your block's diagonal measurement. Cut the square diagonally once to produce two corner triangles.

Easy Floral Appliqué Patterns ~ *Eula Mae Long*

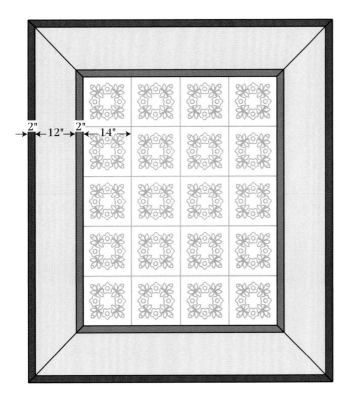

SETTING A. Twenty blocks set straight with multiple plain borders

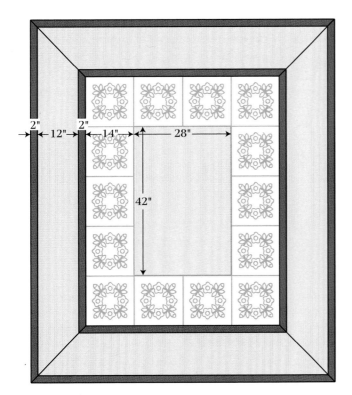

SETTING B. Fourteen blocks set around a rectangular center, with multiple plain borders

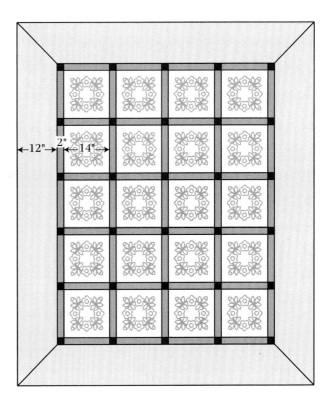

SETTING C. Twenty blocks set straight with sashing and plain border

Eula Mae Long ~ **Easy Floral Appliqué Patterns**

Diagonal Sets

BLOCK SIZE	DIAGONAL
8"	11⅜"
10"	14⅛"
12"	17"
14"	19⅞"
15"	21¼"
16"	22⅝"

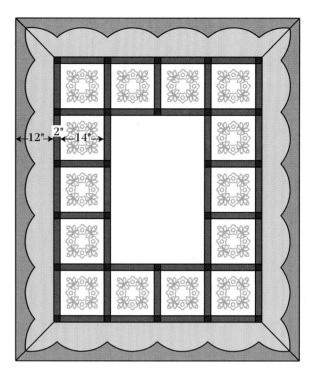

SETTING D. Fourteen blocks set straight with sashing, rectangular center, and swag border

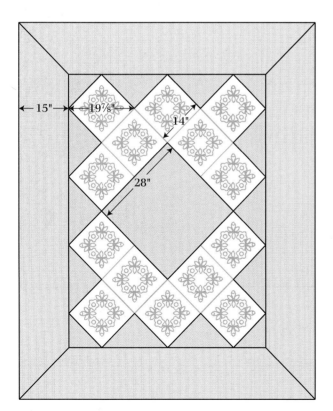

SETTING E. Fourteen blocks set on point around a square center, with plain border

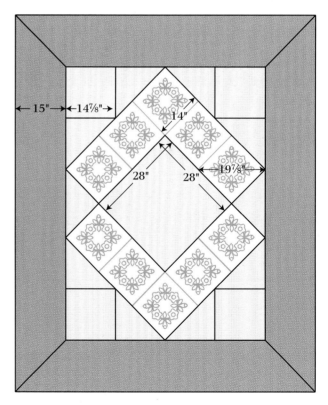

SETTING F. Ten blocks set on point around a square center, with four corner blocks

Choosing Your Fabric

Your fabric choices are important when making a quilt or any fabric project. If you are a beginner, I suggest that you pick a small flowered print that has several of the colors you like. We will call this your "theme fabric." Then pick a palette of fabrics with colors that are in your theme fabric. Choose shades from light to dark in each color. Don't use all plain fabric because your design will be flat with no life. Add dyed fabric, tiny flowers, textured fabrics, and batiks. These will make your design come alive. It's the same with leaf fabrics. Choose many greens, and don't forget to turn the fabric over. Many times you can use the wrong side. Fasten swatches of your selected fabrics to a note card to serve as your fabric reference (fig. 5). Most importantly, buy 100 percent cotton fabric and prewash.

What you buy for the background is just as important as your appliqué fabric. Be sure it is 100 percent cotton and prewash it. There are many beautiful types of fabrics to choose from. If you select muslin, get the best quality because low-quality muslin shrinks a lot. There are many colors in marbleized fabrics, and don't forget tiny prints, dainty yellows, and pale gray. Remember, the background fabric is what shows off your tiny quilting stitches, so take your time with fabric selection. Pass on stiff fabric, no matter how pretty it is. Also be cautious of loosely woven fabric, because you will lose your quilting stitches in this type of fabric.

Fig. 5. Sample theme fabric palette

Assembling Your Supplies

Once you have chosen your fabrics, you will need to assemble the following supplies:

✧ Tracing paper

✧ Template plastic

✧ Scissors: one pair for fabric, one pair for paper, and one small, sharp, pointed pair for appliqué

✧ Thread: white 100 percent cotton for basting, and colors to match the fabric pieces for appliqué. If there is no match, go slightly darker.

✧ Needles: size 10–12

✧ Pins and pincushion

✧ Thimble

✧ Marking pencils: a sharp #2 or fine-pointed mechanical pencil; white, pink, or yellow pencils for marking dark fabric; and a black-leaded template pencil for making templates

✧ Seam ripper

✧ Iron and ironing board

✧ Rotary cutter

✧ Freezer paper, if desired for appliqué

✧ Directional lamp

✧ Sewing machine

Making Paper Patterns

Take extra care in tracing the design you have chosen for your project onto paper. An accurate pattern will make your project easier to sew. For tracing patterns, I suggest you get a large pad of tracing paper from an art store. On a sheet of this paper, mark your 14" square and cut it out. Then fold this square in half horizontally and vertically and mark the creases with dotted lines (fig. 6). Place the paper square over the pattern in the book and trace the design, keeping the dotted lines on your tracing paper properly positioned with the lines in the book. Then go over the traced lines with a black felt-tip pen. Now you have a paper pattern that can be used over and over to trace the designs on the background fabric (fig. 7).

Transfer the pattern to your background squares as follows: If your background fabric is light colored, all you need to do is tape your tracing paper pattern on a sheet of white poster board. Place the background fabric over the pattern, and use a fine-point mechanical pencil to trace the lines. If you draw slightly inside the pattern lines, the appliqué pieces will cover the lines. If the fabric is too dark to see the pattern through it, you will need a light source, such as a window or light table.

Making Appliqué Templates

With a black template pencil or a sharp lead pencil, trace the appliqué pattern pieces onto clear plastic template material. Make a template for every appliqué piece in the block. Do not add seam allowances to the appliqué templates.

Write on every template piece any placement numbers, grain line marks, and the name of the pattern. Place all template pieces in a small, zipper-sealed plastic bag. Mark the plastic bag with the name of the project.

Cutting Appliqué Pieces

Place the template on the right side of the fabric. With a fine-line or very sharp pencil, mark around the template. Leave about ½" of space between tracings. When you are cutting out the appliqué patches, add a ¼" seam allowance by eye. This seam allowance will be the turn-under for the appliqué patch. The appliqué patches can be stored in the plastic bag with the templates.

Choosing an Appliqué Technique

There are many ways to appliqué. If you have a special technique you like, why change it? If you are a beginner, it's best to try many methods. Taking appliqué classes is a great way to learn these methods. When you find one that you really feel comfortable with, stay with it and practice, practice, and practice some more. I suggest doing some type of appliqué at least twice a week or more. As the old saying goes, "Practice makes perfect."

You will notice that some of the patterns have numbered pieces to let you know in what order the pieces are to be appliquéd. To reduce bulk, do not turn under the allowances where one piece fits underneath another.

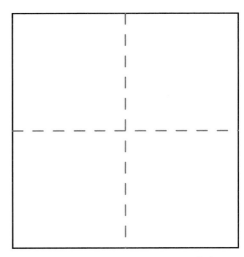

FIG. 6. Prepare a 14" square of the tracing paper.

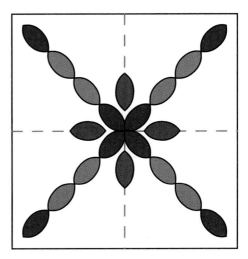

FIG. 7. To trace, align the vertical and horizontal lines with the pattern.

Chapter 2
Floral Appliqué Patterns

You can combine these blocks with each other to make a unique wall or bed quilt. Or, choose one block and repeat it to make a stunning large or small quilt.

ROSE OF SHARON WREATH

ROSE OF SHARON WREATH, 20½" x 20½". Wallhanging made by the author.

placement diagram

Full-sized patterns, on page 17, for 14" block

Grid squares represent 3". Use bias tube for stem
circle. Appliqué the flowers in the order in
which real flowers grow: stems, leaves, flowers.

Rose of Sharon Wreath

bud tip
cut 4

bud
cut 4

leaf
cut 12

flower
cut 4

flower
center
cut 4

*For turned-edge appliqué techniques, add ¼"
turn-under allowances, by eye, as you cut your
fabric pieces.*

WALLHANGING ONE, 39" x 39". Contains Dyana's Daisy, Tania's Tulips, Oregon Beauty, and Cotton Candy. Wall quilt, pieced by the author and machine quilted by Marie Warden, Salem, Oregon. Block patterns on pages 19–23.

placement diagram

Full-sized patterns, on this page, for 14" block

Grid squares represent 3". Stems are made with bias tubes. Appliqué the flowers in the order in which real flowers grow: stems, leaves, flowers.

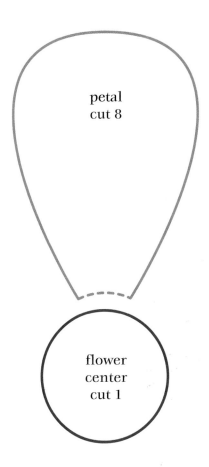

petal
cut 8

flower
center
cut 1

For turned-edge appliqué techniques, add ¼" turn-under allowances, by eye, as you cut your fabric pieces.

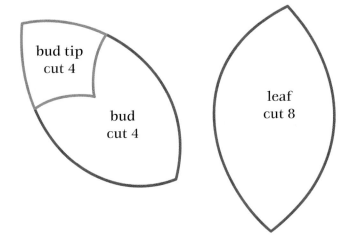

bud tip
cut 4

bud
cut 4

leaf
cut 8

placement diagram
Full-sized patterns, on page 21, for 14" block

Grid squares represent 3". Stems are made with bias tubes. Appliqué the flowers in the order in which real flowers grow: stems, leaves, flowers.

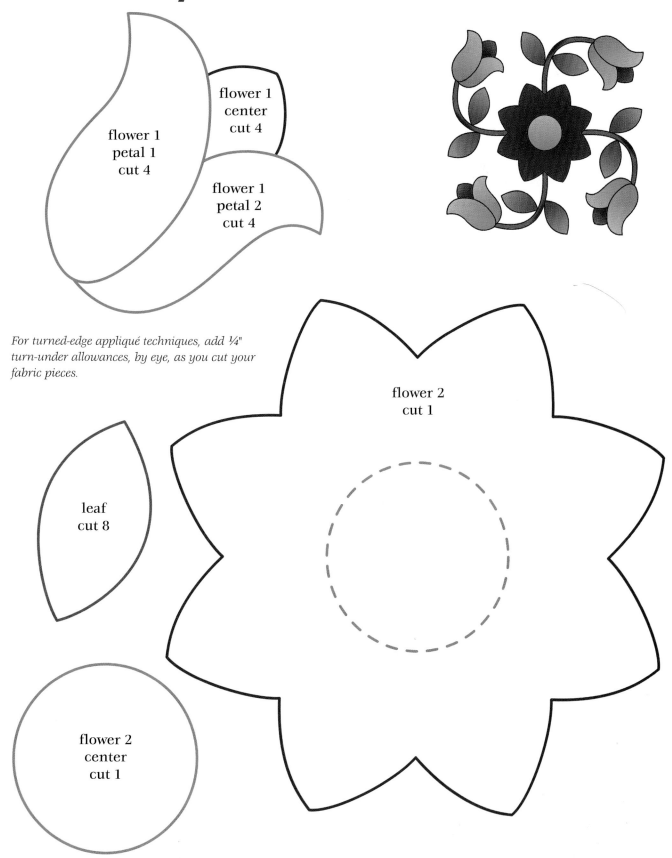

flower 1
center
cut 4

flower 1
petal 1
cut 4

flower 1
petal 2
cut 4

*For turned-edge appliqué techniques, add ¼"
turn-under allowances, by eye, as you cut your
fabric pieces.*

flower 2
cut 1

leaf
cut 8

flower 2
center
cut 1

placement diagram

Full-sized patterns, on this page, for 14" block

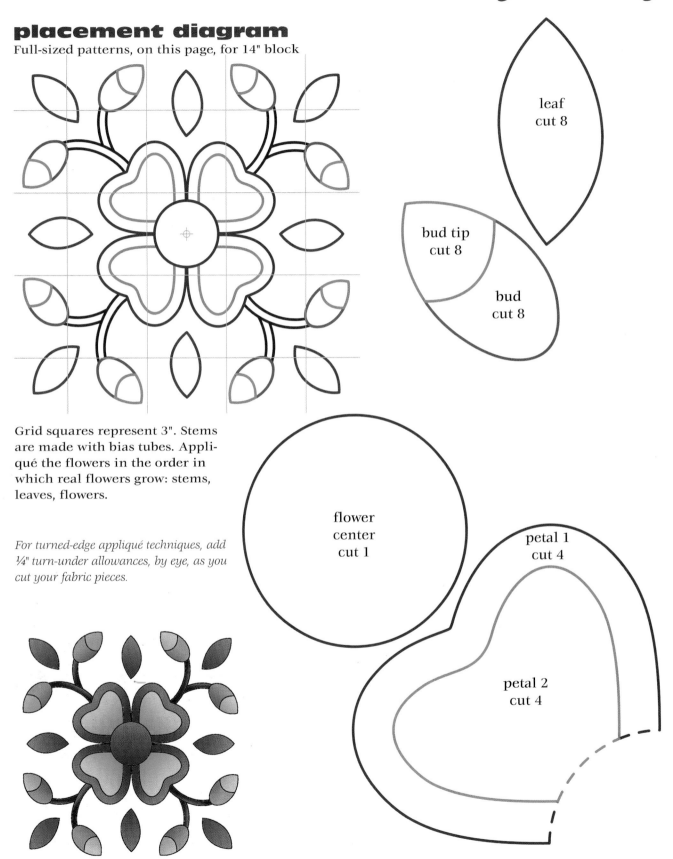

leaf
cut 8

bud tip
cut 8

bud
cut 8

Grid squares represent 3". Stems are made with bias tubes. Appliqué the flowers in the order in which real flowers grow: stems, leaves, flowers.

For turned-edge appliqué techniques, add ¼" turn-under allowances, by eye, as you cut your fabric pieces.

flower
center
cut 1

petal 1
cut 4

petal 2
cut 4

Cotton Candy WALLHANGING ONE

placement diagram

Full-sized patterns, on this page, for 14" block

Grid squares represent 3". Stems are made with bias tubes. Appliqué the flowers in the order in which real flowers grow: stems, leaves, flowers.

leaf
cut 8

For turned-edge appliqué techniques, add ¼" turn-under allowances, by eye, as you cut your fabric pieces.

petal 1
cut 4

petal 2
cut 4

petal 3
cut 4

calyx
cut 4

center
cut 1

WALLHANGING TWO, 36" x 36". Contains Heart of Flowers, Basket of Flowers, Basket of Clematis, and Twirling Tulips. Wall quilt, pieced by the author and quilted by Marie Warden, Salem, Oregon. Block patterns on pages 25–32.

placement diagram
Full-sized patterns, on page 26, for 14" block

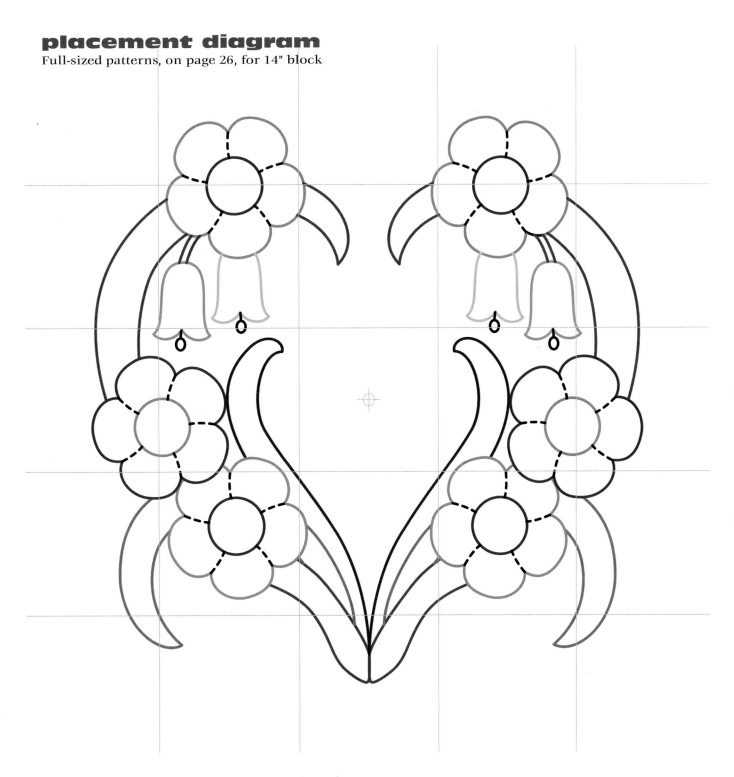

Grid squares represent 3". Stems are made with bias tubes. Appliqué the flowers in the order in which real flowers grow: stems, leaves, flowers.

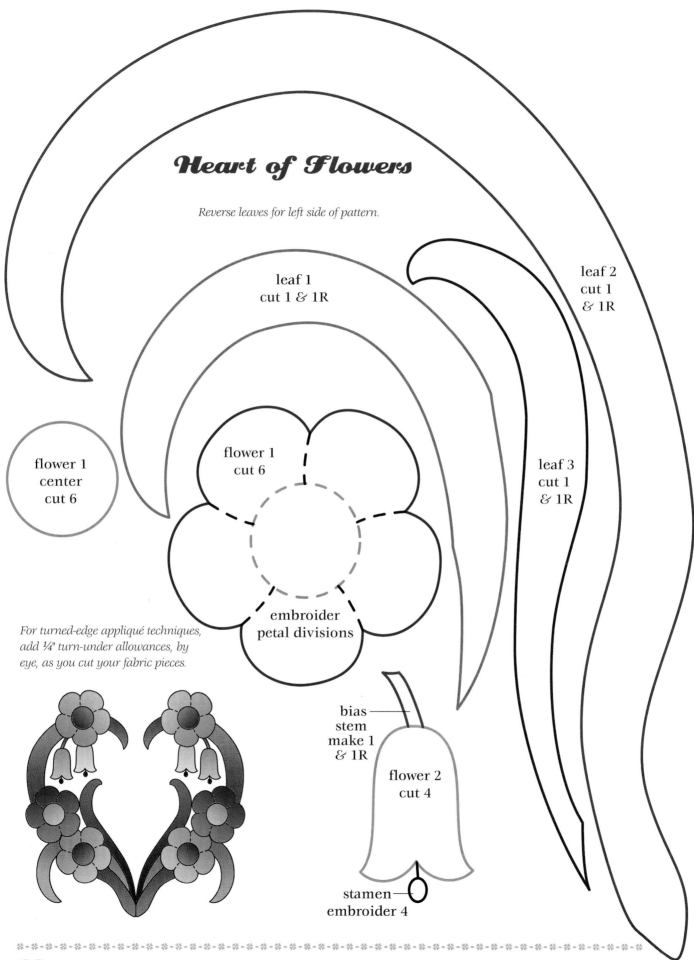

Heart of Flowers

Reverse leaves for left side of pattern.

leaf 1
cut 1 & 1R

leaf 2
cut 1
& 1R

flower 1
center
cut 6

flower 1
cut 6

leaf 3
cut 1
& 1R

embroider
petal divisions

*For turned-edge appliqué techniques,
add ¼" turn-under allowances, by
eye, as you cut your fabric pieces.*

bias
stem
make 1
& 1R

flower 2
cut 4

stamen
embroider 4

Basket of Clematis WALLHANGING TWO

placement diagram
Full-sized patterns, on pages 28–29, for 14" block

Grid squares represent 3". Appliqué the flowers in the order in which real flowers grow: leaves then flowers.

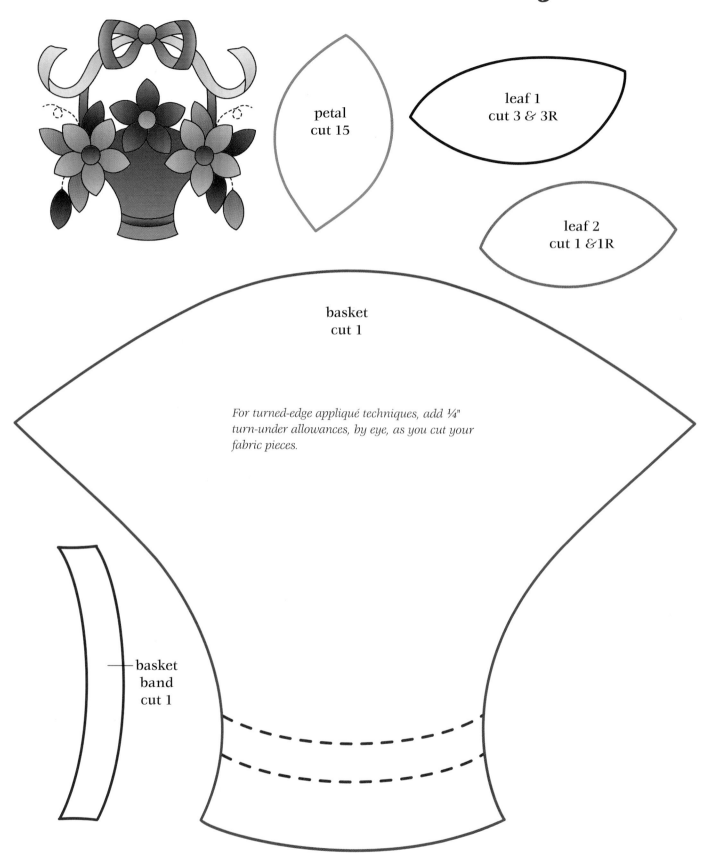

petal
cut 15

leaf 1
cut 3 & 3R

leaf 2
cut 1 & 1R

basket
cut 1

*For turned-edge appliqué techniques, add ¼"
turn-under allowances, by eye, as you cut your
fabric pieces.*

basket
band
cut 1

Basket of Clematis WALLHANGING TWO

petal pattern
on page 28
make 3 flowers

flower
center
cut 3

leaf 1

basket handle
cut 1 & 1R

leaf 1

embroider
tendrils

leaf 2

embroider
stems

leaf 1

*For turned-edge appliqué techniques, add ¼"
turn-under allowances, by eye, as you cut your
fabric pieces.*

bow
cut 1 & 1R

bow
center
cut 1

ribbon
cut 1 & 1R

bow
cut 1
& 1R

bow
cut 1
& 1R

ribbon
cut 1
& 1R

ribbon
cut 1 & 1R

placement diagram

Full-sized patterns, on page 31, for 14" block

Grid squares represent 3". Appliqué the flowers
in the order in which real flowers grow: leaves
then flowers.

Basket of Flowers WALLHANGING TWO

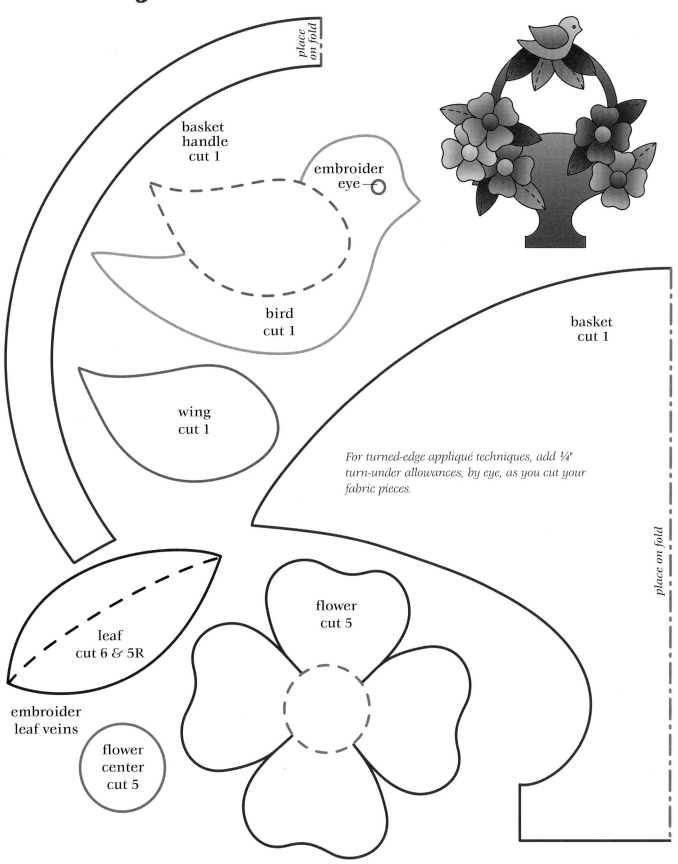

place on fold

basket
handle
cut 1

embroider
eye —◯

bird
cut 1

basket
cut 1

wing
cut 1

*For turned-edge appliqué techniques, add ¼"
turn-under allowances, by eye, as you cut your
fabric pieces.*

place on fold

flower
cut 5

leaf
cut 6 & 5R

embroider
leaf veins

flower
center
cut 5

placement diagram

Full-sized patterns, on this page, for 14" block

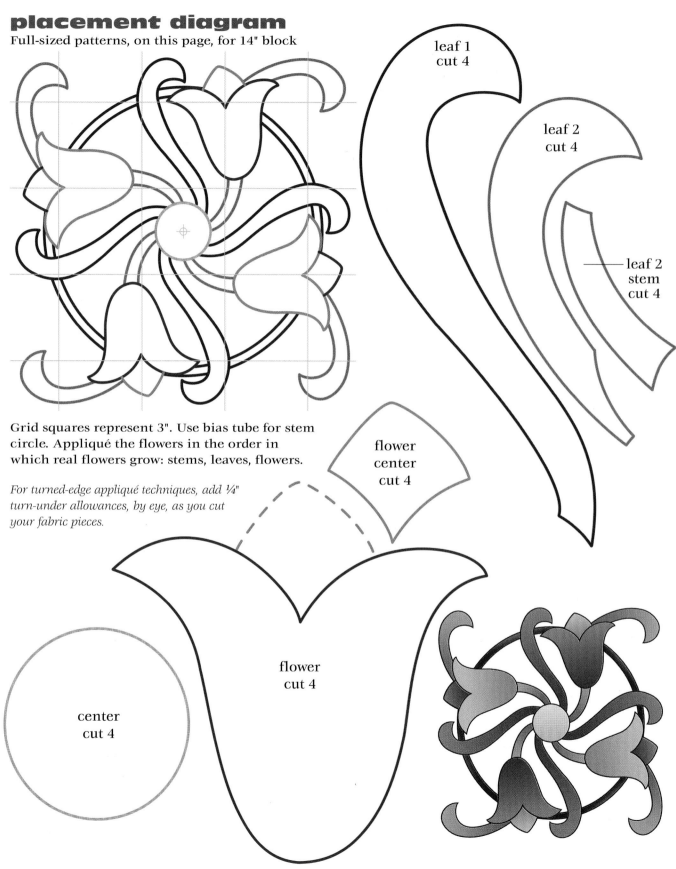

leaf 1
cut 4

leaf 2
cut 4

leaf 2
stem
cut 4

flower
center
cut 4

Grid squares represent 3". Use bias tube for stem circle. Appliqué the flowers in the order in which real flowers grow: stems, leaves, flowers.

For turned-edge appliqué techniques, add ¼" turn-under allowances, by eye, as you cut your fabric pieces.

flower
cut 4

center
cut 4

PETUNIA WREATH

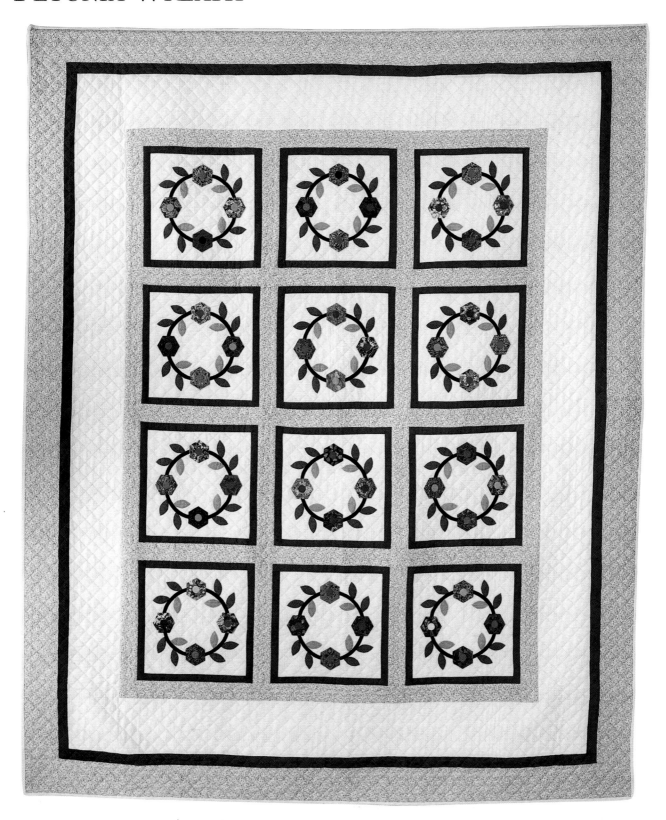

PETUNIA WREATH, 84" x 100". Bed quilt, pieced by the author and hand quilted by Edna Buhler, Salem, Oregon. Block pattern on page 34.

placement diagram
Full-sized patterns, on this page, for 14" block

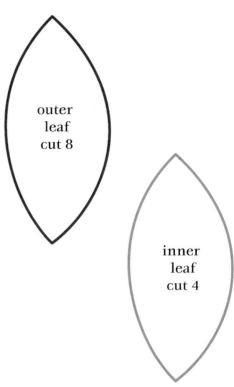

outer
leaf
cut 8

inner
leaf
cut 4

Grid squares represent 3". Use bias tubes for
stem circle. Appliqué the flowers in the order in
which real flowers grow: stems, leaves, flowers.

*For turned-edge appliqué techniques, add ¼"
turn-under allowances, by eye, as you cut your
fabric pieces.*

flower
center
cut 4

flower
cut 4

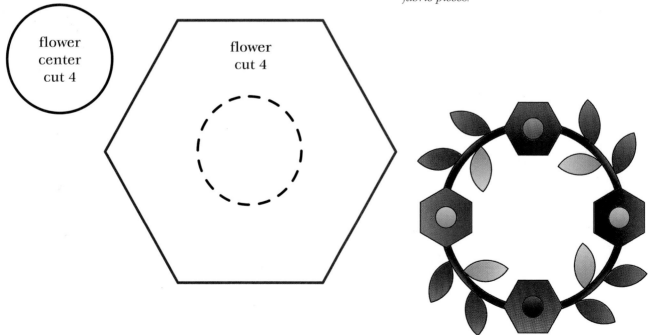

SCRAPPY TULIPS

SCRAPPY TULIPS, 84" x 100". Bed quilt, pieced by the author and hand quilted by Edna Buhler, Salem, Oregon. Block pattern on page 36–37.

placement diagram

Full-sized patterns, on pages 36-37, for 14" block

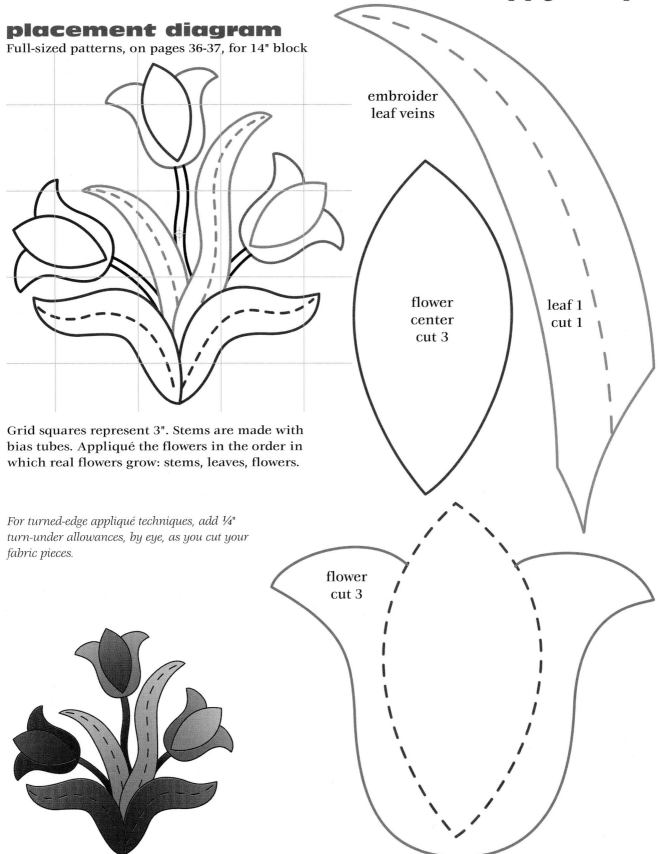

embroider
leaf veins

flower
center
cut 3

leaf 1
cut 1

flower
cut 3

Grid squares represent 3". Stems are made with bias tubes. Appliqué the flowers in the order in which real flowers grow: stems, leaves, flowers.

For turned-edge appliqué techniques, add ¼" turn-under allowances, by eye, as you cut your fabric pieces.

Scrappy Tulips

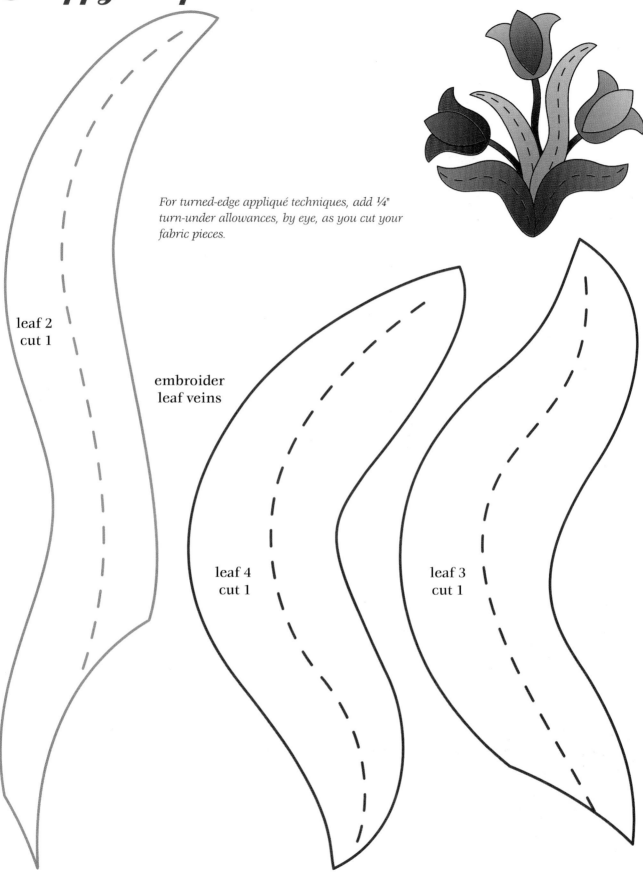

*For turned-edge appliqué techniques, add ¼"
turn-under allowances, by eye, as you cut your
fabric pieces.*

leaf 2
cut 1

embroider
leaf veins

leaf 4
cut 1

leaf 3
cut 1

TOMORROW'S HEIRLOOM, 84" x 98". Bed quilt,
pieced by the author and hand quilted by Edna Buhler,
Salem, Oregon. Block patterns on pages 39–75.

placement diagram
Full-sized patterns, on page 40, for 14" block

Grid squares represent 3". Stems are made with bias tubes. Appliqué the flowers in the order in which real flowers grow: stems, leaves, flowers.

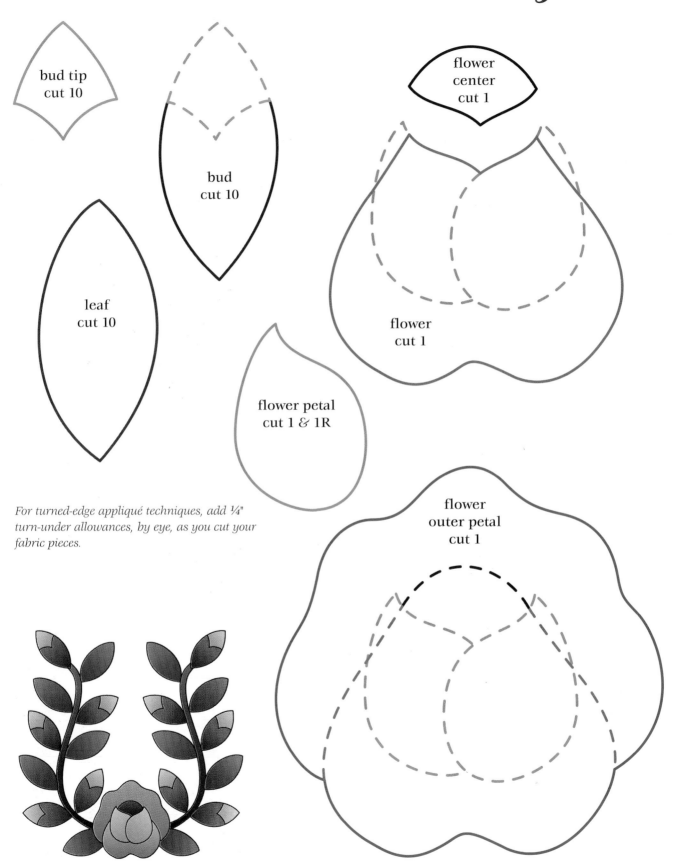

bud tip
cut 10

bud
cut 10

flower
center
cut 1

leaf
cut 10

flower
cut 1

flower petal
cut 1 & 1R

*For turned-edge appliqué techniques, add ¼"
turn-under allowances, by eye, as you cut your
fabric pieces.*

flower
outer petal
cut 1

placement diagram

Full-sized patterns, on pages 41–42, for 14" block

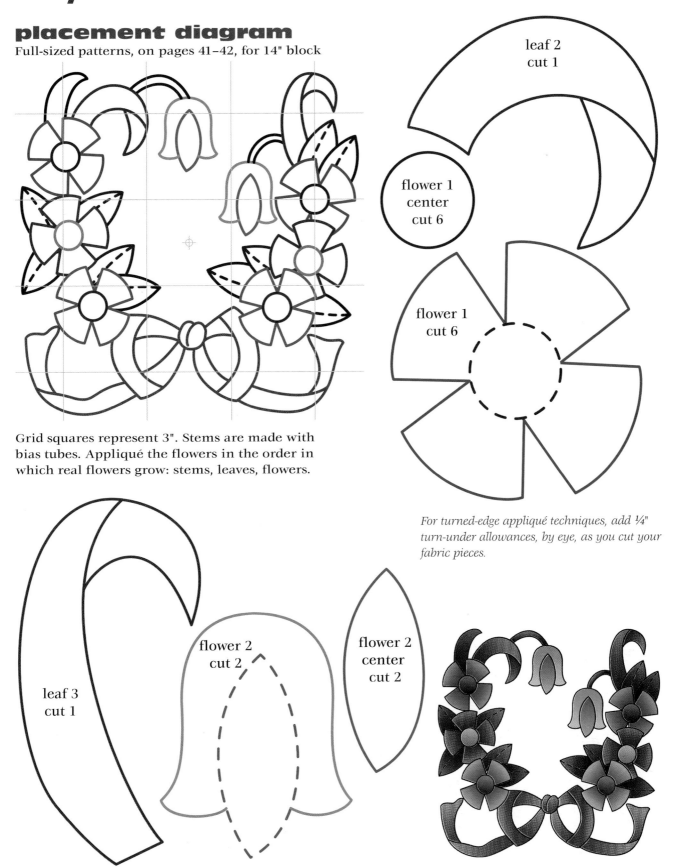

Grid squares represent 3". Stems are made with bias tubes. Appliqué the flowers in the order in which real flowers grow: stems, leaves, flowers.

leaf 2
cut 1

flower 1
center
cut 6

flower 1
cut 6

For turned-edge appliqué techniques, add ¼" turn-under allowances, by eye, as you cut your fabric pieces.

leaf 3
cut 1

flower 2
cut 2

flower 2
center
cut 2

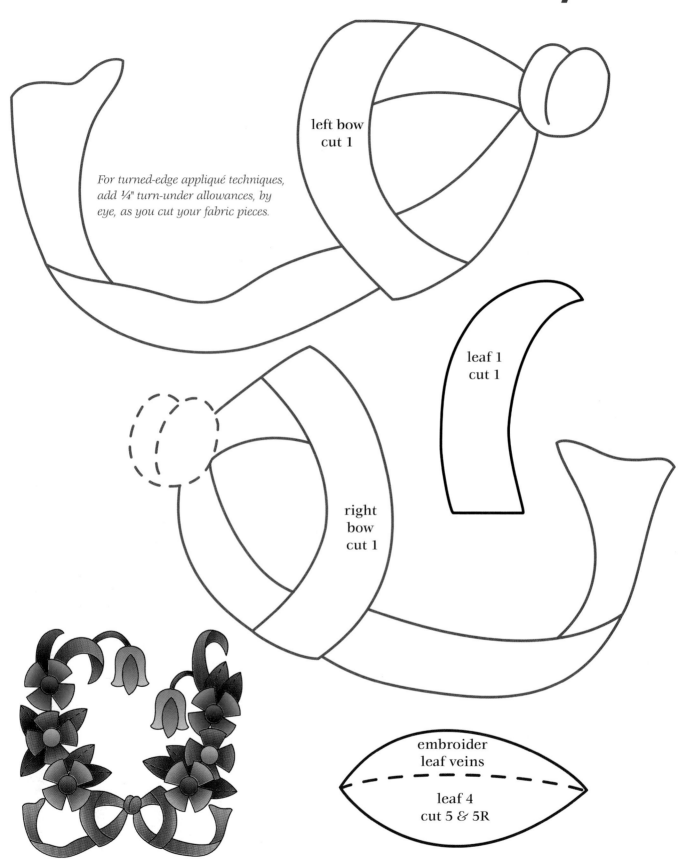

For turned-edge appliqué techniques, add ¼" turn-under allowances, by eye, as you cut your fabric pieces.

left bow
cut 1

leaf 1
cut 1

right
bow
cut 1

embroider
leaf veins

leaf 4
cut 5 & 5R

placement diagram

Full-sized patterns, on this page, for 14" block

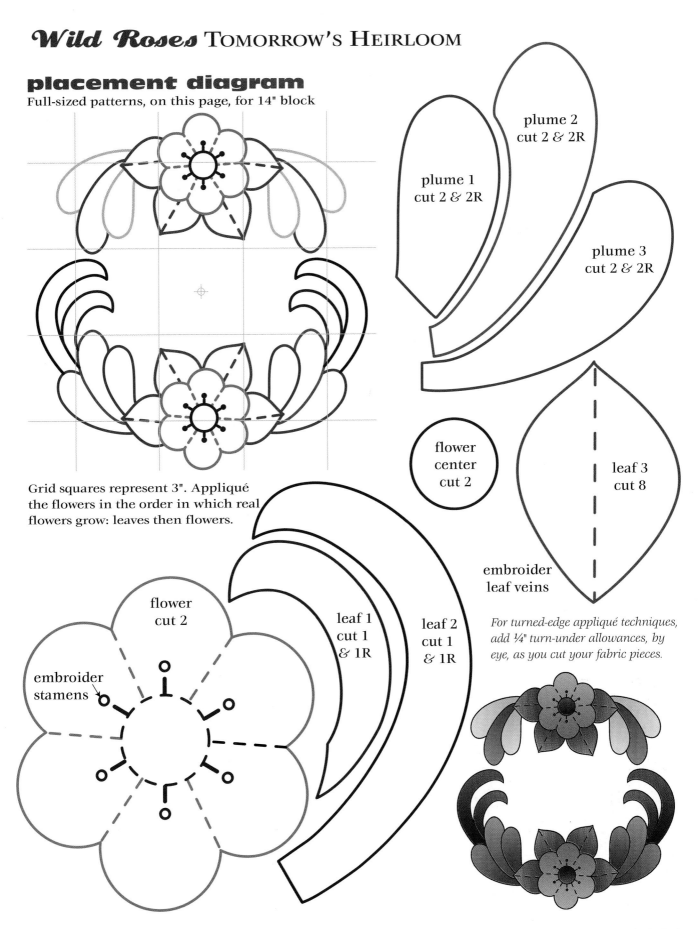

plume 2
cut 2 & 2R

plume 1
cut 2 & 2R

plume 3
cut 2 & 2R

Grid squares represent 3". Appliqué
the flowers in the order in which real
flowers grow: leaves then flowers.

flower
center
cut 2

leaf 3
cut 8

embroider
leaf veins

flower
cut 2

leaf 1
cut 1
& 1R

leaf 2
cut 1
& 1R

embroider
stamens

*For turned-edge appliqué techniques,
add ¼" turn-under allowances, by
eye, as you cut your fabric pieces.*

placement diagram
Full-sized patterns, on page 45, for 14" block

Grid squares represent 3". Appliqué the flowers
in the order in which real flowers grow: leaves
then flowers.

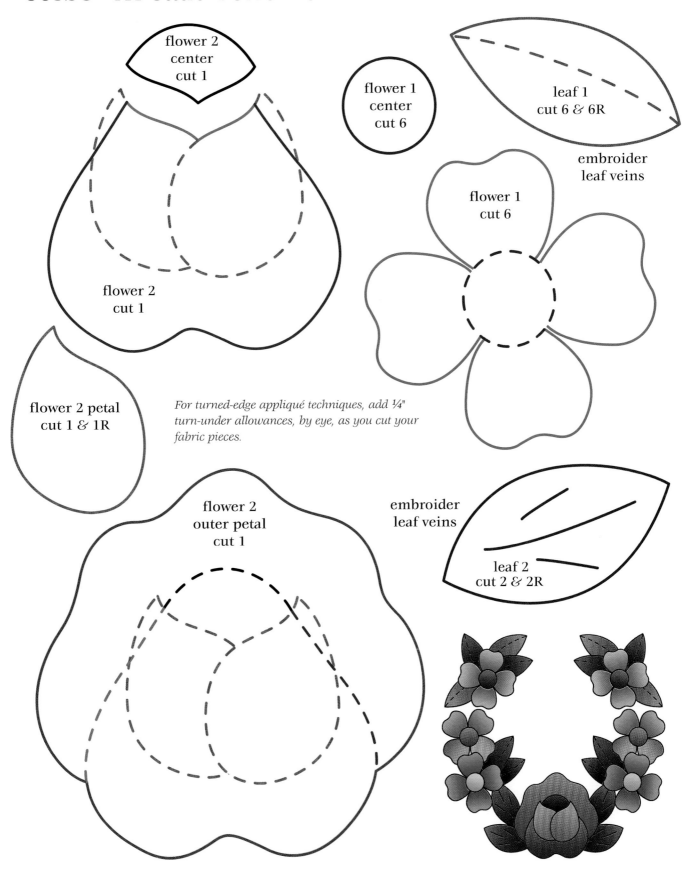

flower 2
center
cut 1

flower 1
center
cut 6

leaf 1
cut 6 & 6R

embroider
leaf veins

flower 1
cut 6

flower 2
cut 1

flower 2 petal
cut 1 & 1R

*For turned-edge appliqué techniques, add ¼"
turn-under allowances, by eye, as you cut your
fabric pieces.*

flower 2
outer petal
cut 1

embroider
leaf veins

leaf 2
cut 2 & 2R

placement diagram

Full-sized patterns, on pages 46–47, for 14" block

Grid squares represent 3". Stems are made with bias tubes. Appliqué the flowers in the order in which real flowers grow: stems, leaves, flowers.

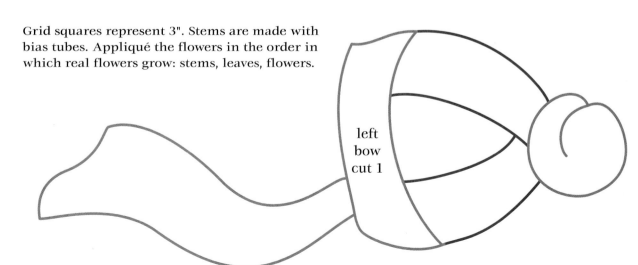

left
bow
cut 1

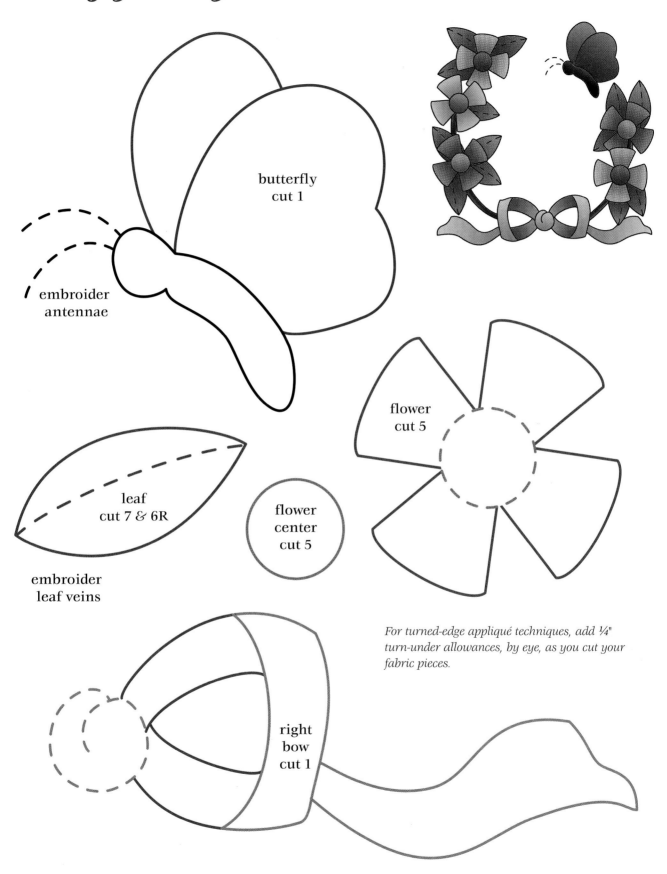

butterfly
cut 1

embroider
antennae

flower
cut 5

leaf
cut 7 & 6R

flower
center
cut 5

embroider
leaf veins

For turned-edge appliqué techniques, add ¼"
turn-under allowances, by eye, as you cut your
fabric pieces.

right
bow
cut 1

placement diagram
Full-sized patterns, on page 49, for 14" block

Grid squares represent 3". Stems are made with
bias tubes. Appliqué the flowers in the order in
which real flowers grow: stems, leaves, flowers.

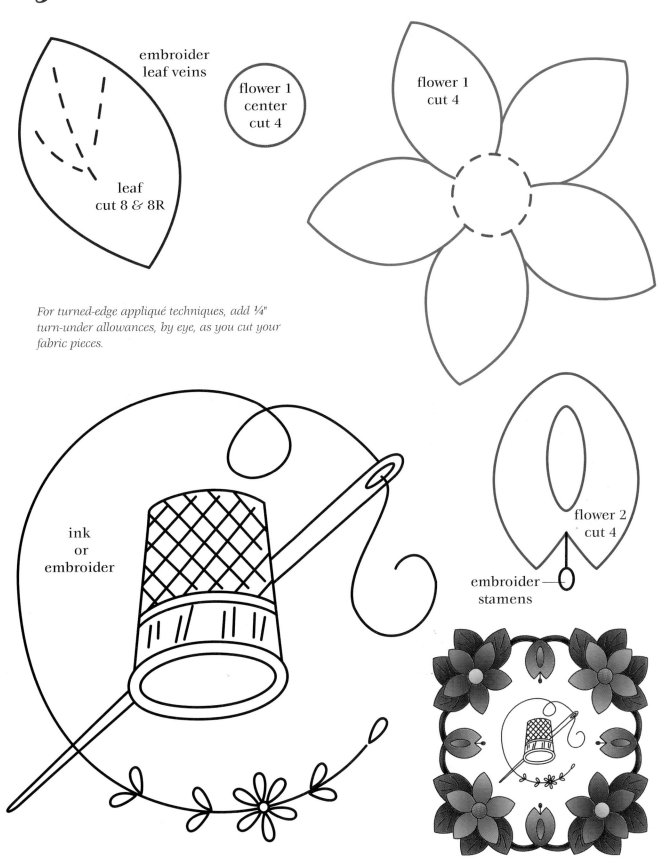

Signature Block TOMORROW'S HEIRLOOM

embroider
leaf veins

flower 1
center
cut 4

flower 1
cut 4

leaf
cut 8 & 8R

*For turned-edge appliqué techniques, add ¼"
turn-under allowances, by eye, as you cut your
fabric pieces.*

ink
or
embroider

flower 2
cut 4

embroider
stamens

placement diagram
Full-sized patterns, on page 51, for 14" block

Grid squares represent 3". Stems are made with bias tubes. Appliqué the flowers in the order in which real flowers grow: stems, leaves, flowers.

Easy Floral Appliqué Patterns ~ *Eula Mae Long*

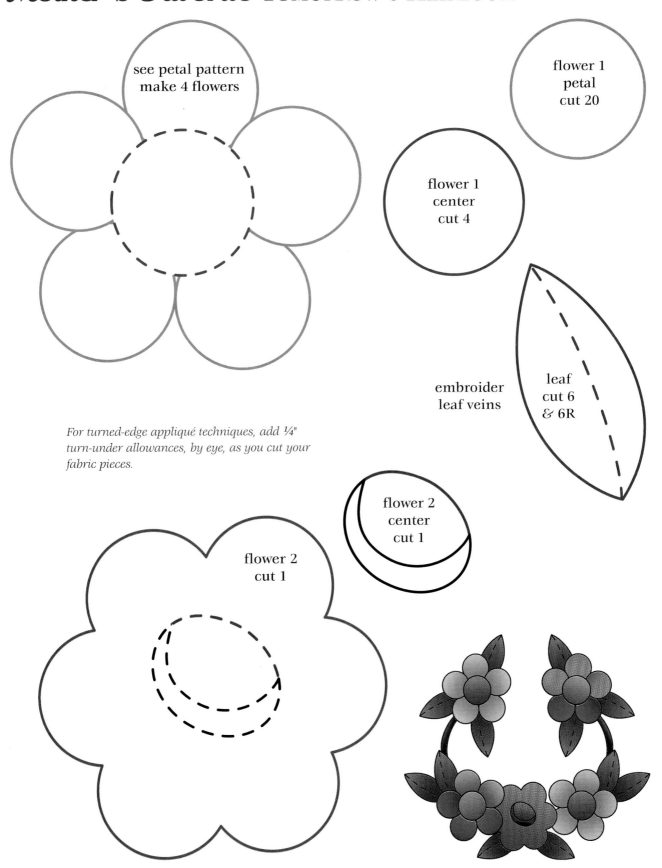

see petal pattern
make 4 flowers

flower 1
petal
cut 20

flower 1
center
cut 4

embroider
leaf veins

leaf
cut 6
& 6R

*For turned-edge appliqué techniques, add ¼"
turn-under allowances, by eye, as you cut your
fabric pieces.*

flower 2
center
cut 1

flower 2
cut 1

placement diagram
Full-sized patterns, on page 53, for 14" block

Grid squares represent 3". Stems are made with
bias tubes. Appliqué the flowers in the order in
which real flowers grow: stems, leaves, flowers.

Bow and Flowers TOMORROW'S HEIRLOOM

bow
cut 1
& 1R

leaf 1
cut 6
& 6R

leaf 2
cut 1
& 1R

embroider
leaf veins

leaf 3
cut 1 & 1R

*For turned-edge appliqué techniques, add ¼"
turn-under allowances, by eye, as you cut your
fabric pieces.*

flower 1
center
cut 8

flower 1
cut 8

flower 2
center
cut 1

flower 2
cut 1

placement diagram
Full-sized patterns, on this page, for 14" block

Grid squares represent 3". Stems are made with bias tubes. Appliqué the flowers in the order in which real flowers grow: stems, leaves, flowers.

For turned-edge appliqué techniques, add ¼" turn-under allowances, by eye, as you cut your fabric pieces.

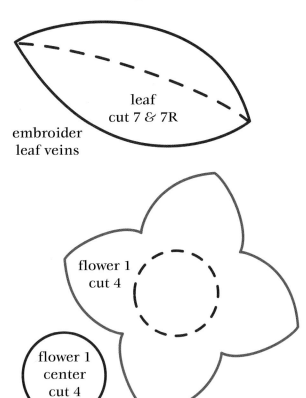

leaf
cut 7 & 7R

embroider
leaf veins

flower 1
cut 4

flower 1
center
cut 4

flower 2
center
cut 2

flower 2
cut 2

placement diagram

Full-sized patterns, on this page, for 14" block

Grid squares represent 3". Stems are made with bias tubes. Appliqué the flowers in the order in which real flowers grow: stems, leaves, flowers.

For turned-edge appliqué techniques, add ¼" turn-under allowances, by eye, as you cut your fabric pieces.

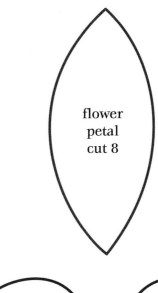

flower
petal
cut 8

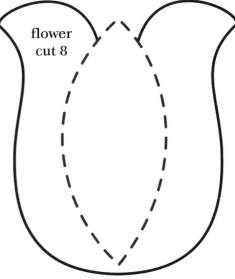

flower
cut 8

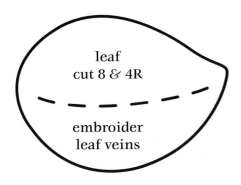

leaf
cut 8 & 4R

embroider
leaf veins

placement diagram

Full-sized patterns, on this page, for 14" block

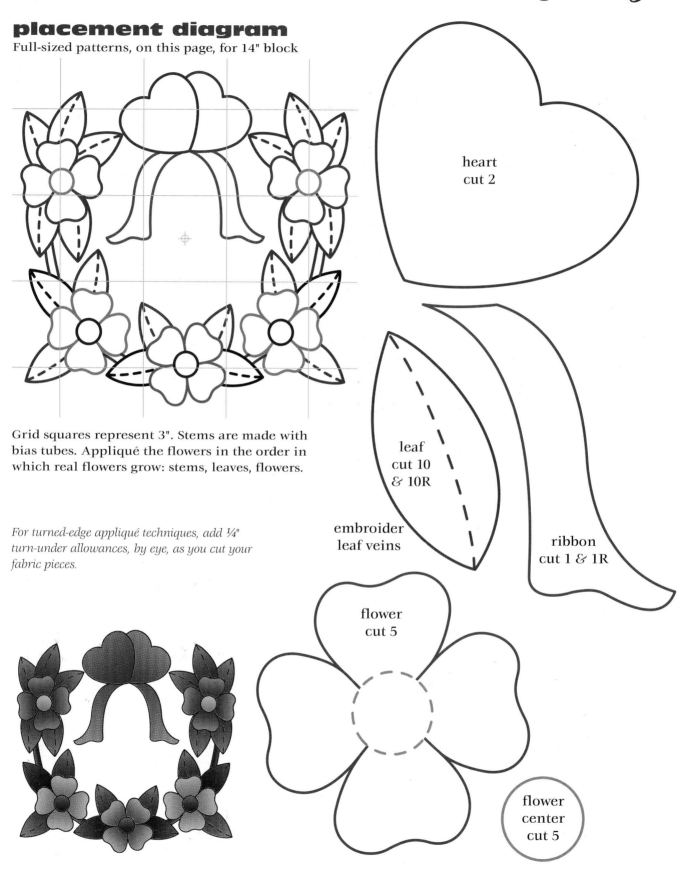

Grid squares represent 3". Stems are made with bias tubes. Appliqué the flowers in the order in which real flowers grow: stems, leaves, flowers.

For turned-edge appliqué techniques, add ¼" turn-under allowances, by eye, as you cut your fabric pieces.

heart
cut 2

leaf
cut 10
& 10R

embroider
leaf veins

ribbon
cut 1 & 1R

flower
cut 5

flower
center
cut 5

placement diagram

Full-sized patterns, on this page, for 14" block

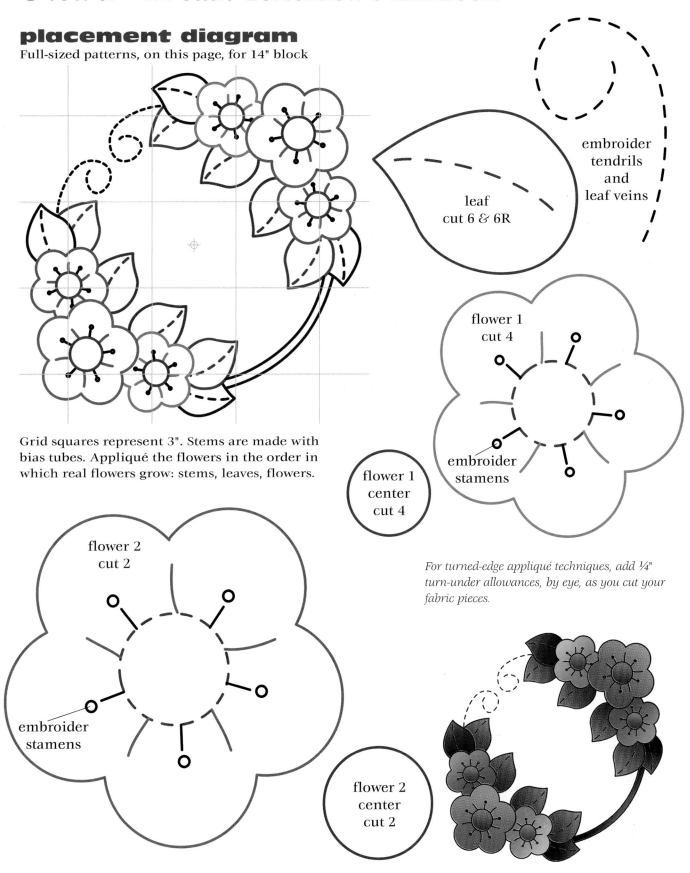

Grid squares represent 3". Stems are made with bias tubes. Appliqué the flowers in the order in which real flowers grow: stems, leaves, flowers.

embroider tendrils and leaf veins

leaf
cut 6 & 6R

flower 1
cut 4

embroider
stamens

flower 1
center
cut 4

For turned-edge appliqué techniques, add ¼" turn-under allowances, by eye, as you cut your fabric pieces.

flower 2
cut 2

embroider
stamens

flower 2
center
cut 2

placement diagram

Full-sized patterns, on this page, for 14" block

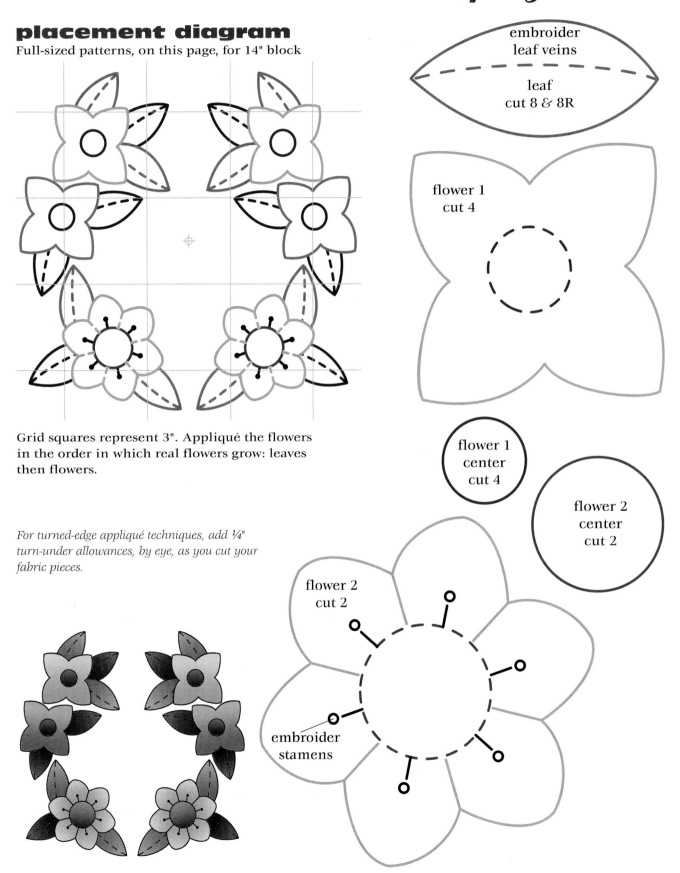

Grid squares represent 3". Appliqué the flowers in the order in which real flowers grow: leaves then flowers.

For turned-edge appliqué techniques, add ¼" turn-under allowances, by eye, as you cut your fabric pieces.

embroider leaf veins

leaf
cut 8 & 8R

flower 1
cut 4

flower 1
center
cut 4

flower 2
center
cut 2

flower 2
cut 2

embroider
stamens

placement diagram
Full-sized patterns, on page 60, for 14" block

Grid squares represent 3". Stems are made with bias tubes. Appliqué the flowers in the order in which real flowers grow: stems, leaves, flowers.

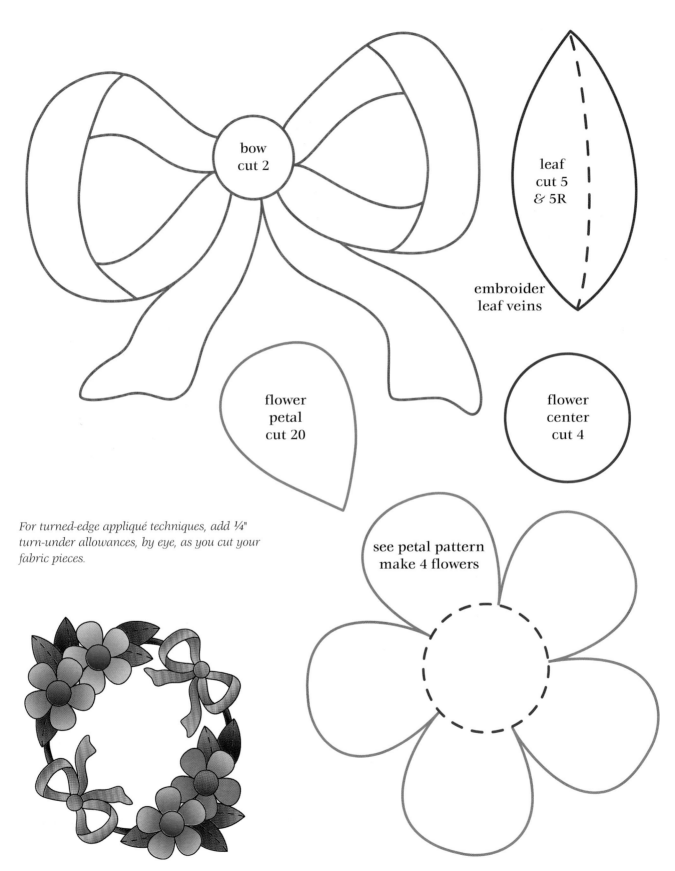

bow
cut 2

leaf
cut 5
& 5R

embroider
leaf veins

flower
petal
cut 20

flower
center
cut 4

see petal pattern
make 4 flowers

*For turned-edge appliqué techniques, add ¼"
turn-under allowances, by eye, as you cut your
fabric pieces.*

placement diagram
Full-sized patterns, on page 62, for 14" block

Grid squares represent 3". Stems are made with bias tubes. Appliqué the flowers in the order in which real flowers grow: stems, leaves, flowers.

flower 2
cut 1

flower 2
center
cut 1

leaf 1
cut 3 & 3R

embroider
stamens
and leaf veins

bud tip
cut 1 & 1R

bud
cut 1 & 1R

leaf 2
cut 3 & 3R

*For turned-edge appliqué techniques, add ¼"
turn-under allowances, by eye, as you cut your
fabric pieces.*

embroider
tendrils

flower 1
cut 3

placement diagram
Full-sized patterns, on page 64, for 14" block

Grid squares represent 3". Stems are made with bias tubes. Appliqué the flowers in the order in which real flowers grow: stems, leaves, flowers.

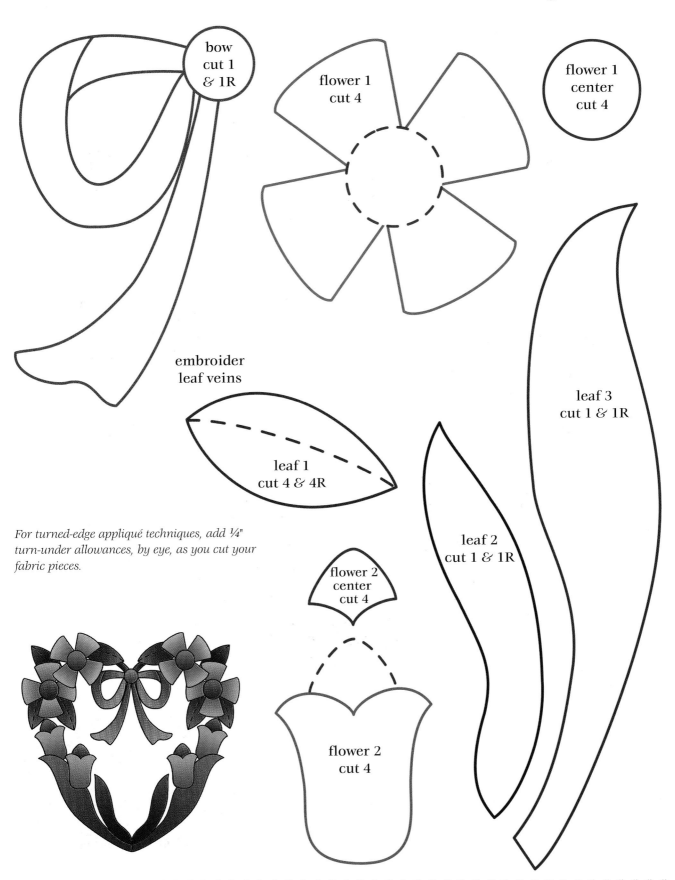

bow
cut 1
& 1R

flower 1
cut 4

flower 1
center
cut 4

embroider
leaf veins

leaf 3
cut 1 & 1R

leaf 1
cut 4 & 4R

*For turned-edge appliqué techniques, add ¼"
turn-under allowances, by eye, as you cut your
fabric pieces.*

flower 2
center
cut 4

leaf 2
cut 1 & 1R

flower 2
cut 4

Spring Bouquet TOMORROW'S HEIRLOOM

placement diagram

Full-sized patterns, on pages 65–67, for 14" block

flower 1
cut 1
& 1R

flower 1
center
cut 1
& 1R

For turned-edge appliqué techniques, add ¼" turn-under allowances, by eye, as you cut your fabric pieces.

bud tip
cut 1

bud
cut 1

Grid squares represent 3". Appliqué the flowers in the order in which real flowers grow: leaves then flowers.

leaf 2
cut 1

leaf 3
cut 1

leaf 1
cut 1

bow
cut 1

leaf 4
cut 4
& 4R

embroider
leaf veins

*For turned-edge appliqué techniques, add ¼"
turn-under allowances, by eye, as you cut your
fabric pieces.*

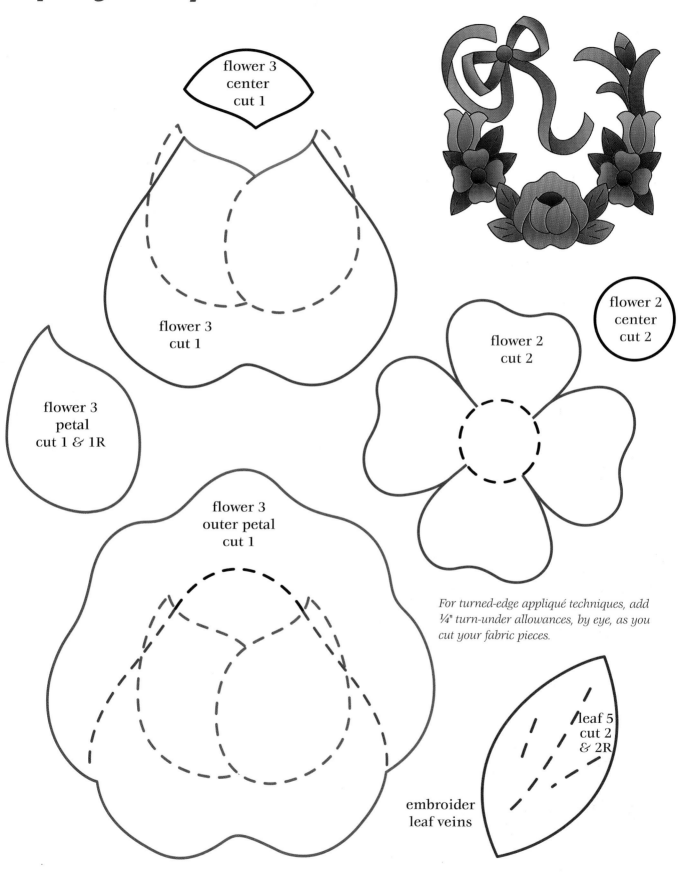

flower 3
center
cut 1

flower 3
cut 1

flower 2
center
cut 2

flower 2
cut 2

flower 3
petal
cut 1 & 1R

flower 3
outer petal
cut 1

For turned-edge appliqué techniques, add ¼" turn-under allowances, by eye, as you cut your fabric pieces.

leaf 5
cut 2
& 2R

embroider
leaf veins

placement diagram

Full-sized patterns, on page 69, for 14" block

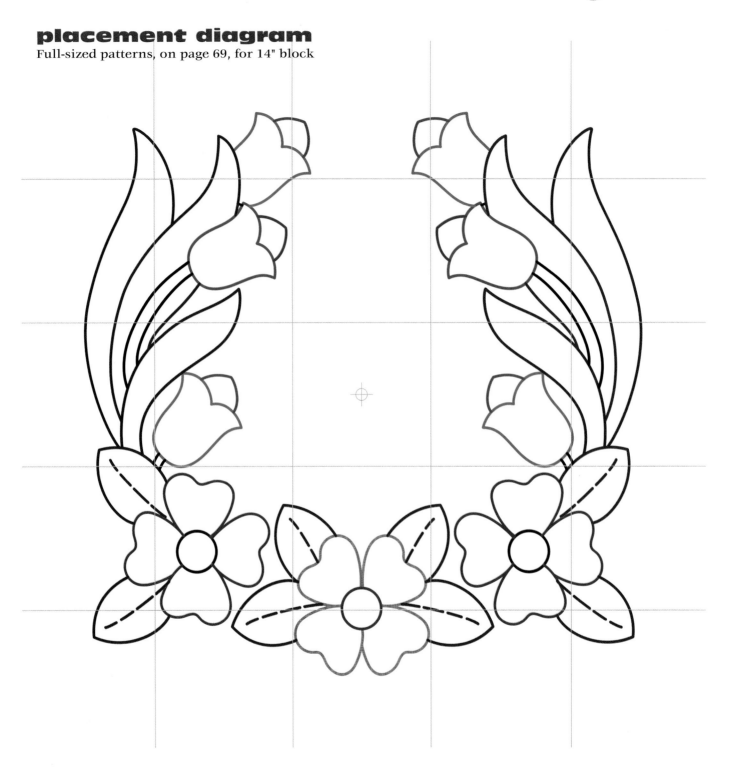

Grid squares represent 3". Stems are made with bias tubes. Appliqué the flowers in the order in which real flowers grow: stems, leaves, flowers.

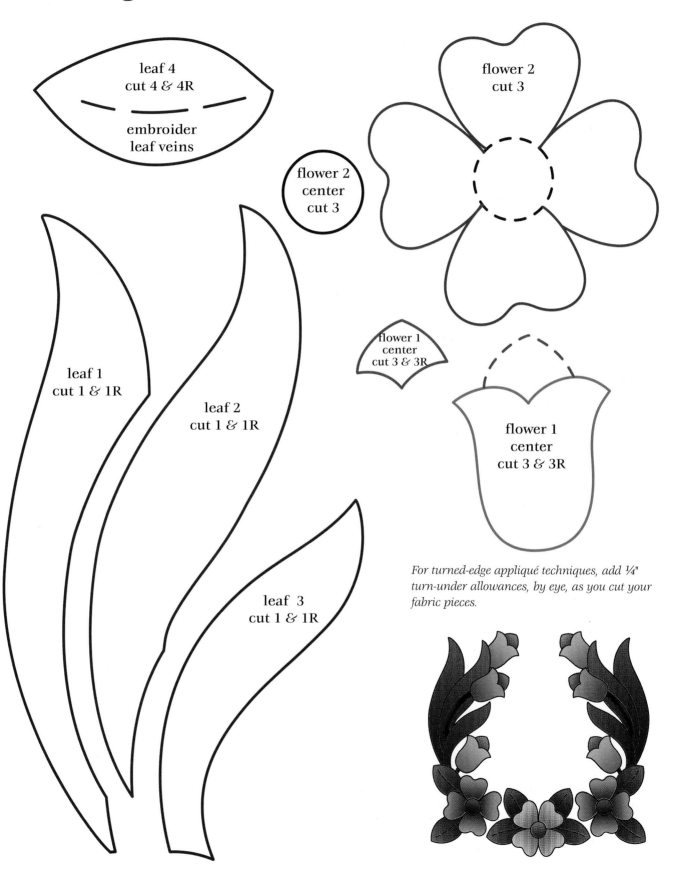

leaf 4
cut 4 & 4R

embroider
leaf veins

flower 2
cut 3

flower 2
center
cut 3

leaf 1
cut 1 & 1R

leaf 2
cut 1 & 1R

flower 1
center
cut 3 & 3R

flower 1
center
cut 3 & 3R

leaf 3
cut 1 & 1R

*For turned-edge appliqué techniques, add ¼"
turn-under allowances, by eye, as you cut your
fabric pieces.*

placement diagram

Full-sized patterns, on pages 70–71, for 14" block

flower
center
cut 6

flower
petal
cut 30

see petal pattern
make 6 flowers

Grid squares represent 3". Stems are made with bias tubes. Appliqué the flowers in the order in which real flowers grow: stems, leaves, flowers.

For turned-edge appliqué techniques, add ¼" turn-under allowances, by eye, as you cut your fabric pieces.

Easy Floral Appliqué Patterns ~ *Eula Mae Long*

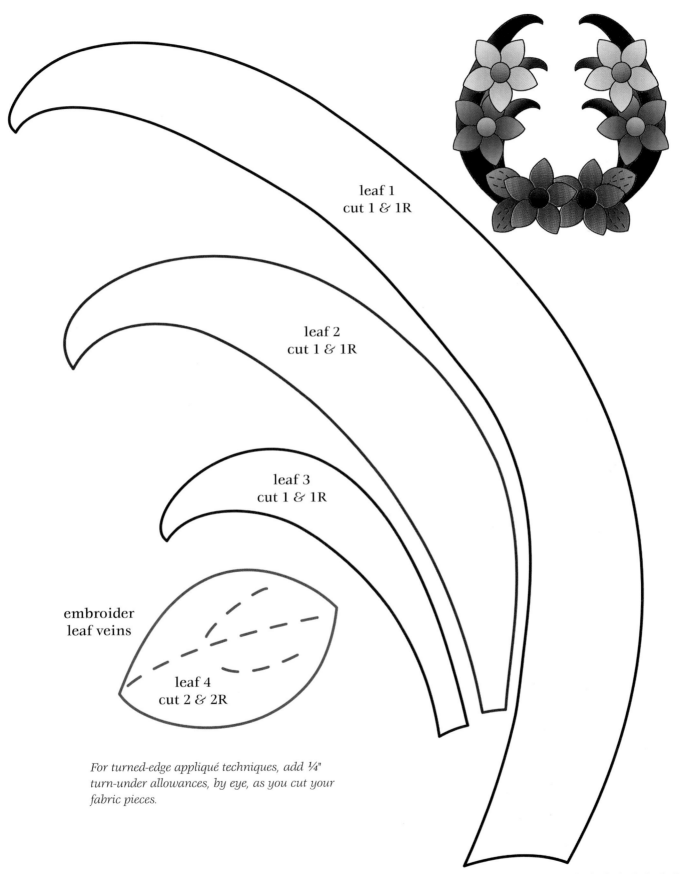

leaf 1
cut 1 & 1R

leaf 2
cut 1 & 1R

leaf 3
cut 1 & 1R

embroider
leaf veins

leaf 4
cut 2 & 2R

For turned-edge appliqué techniques, add ¼"
turn-under allowances, by eye, as you cut your
fabric pieces.

placement diagram

Full-sized patterns, on pages 72–73, for 14" block

Grid squares represent 3". Appliqué the flowers in the order in which real flowers grow: leaves then flowers.

For turned-edge appliqué techniques, add ¼" turn-under allowances, by eye, as you cut your fabric pieces.

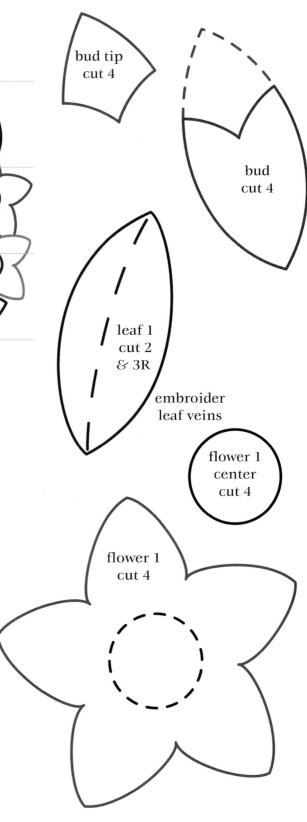

bud tip
cut 4

bud
cut 4

leaf 1
cut 2
& 3R

embroider
leaf veins

flower 1
center
cut 4

flower 1
cut 4

Easy Floral Appliqué Patterns ~ *Eula Mae Long*

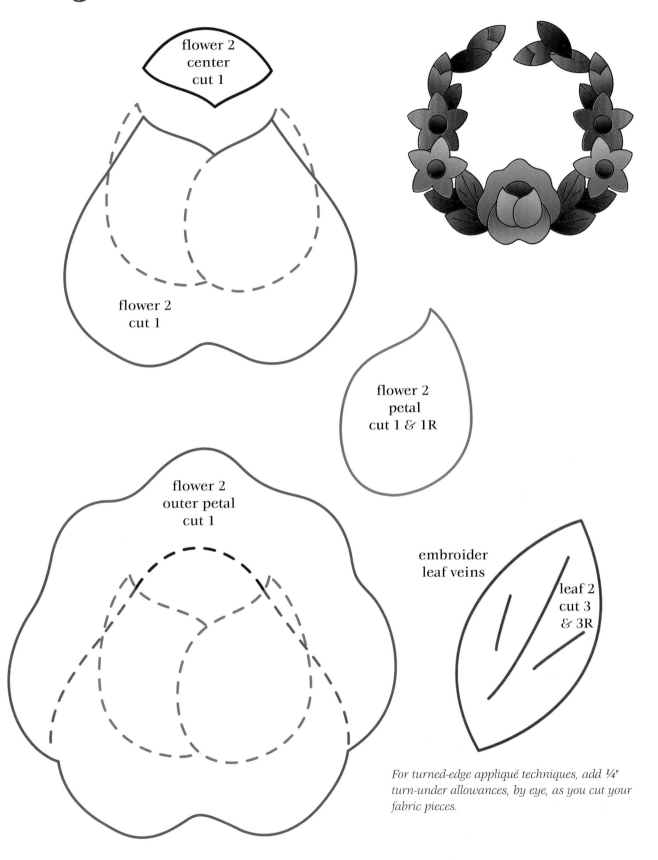

flower 2
center
cut 1

flower 2
cut 1

flower 2
petal
cut 1 & 1R

flower 2
outer petal
cut 1

embroider
leaf veins

leaf 2
cut 3
& 3R

*For turned-edge appliqué techniques, add ¼"
turn-under allowances, by eye, as you cut your
fabric pieces.*

TOMORROW'S HEIRLOOM *Swag Border*

Swag border pattern for TOMORROW'S HEIRLOOM *on page 38*

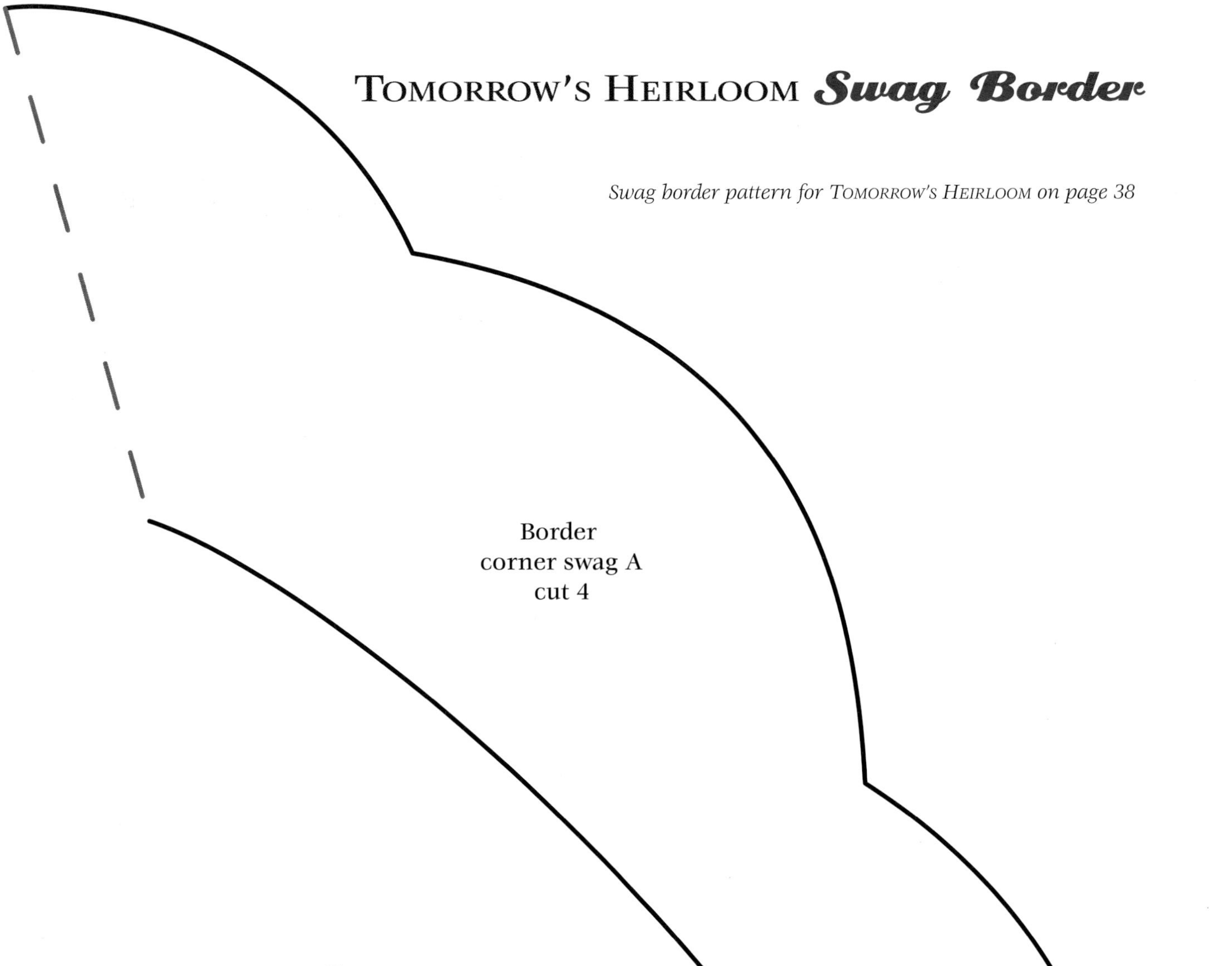

Border
corner swag A
cut 4

placement diagram

Full-sized patterns on pages 74–75

Grid squares represent 3". Appliqué swag first,
then flowers.

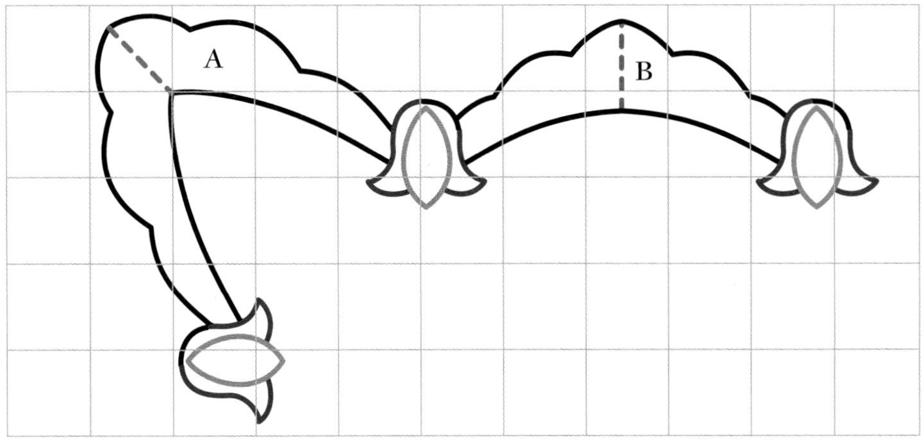

A

B

Easy Floral Appliqué Patterns ~ *Eula Mae Long*

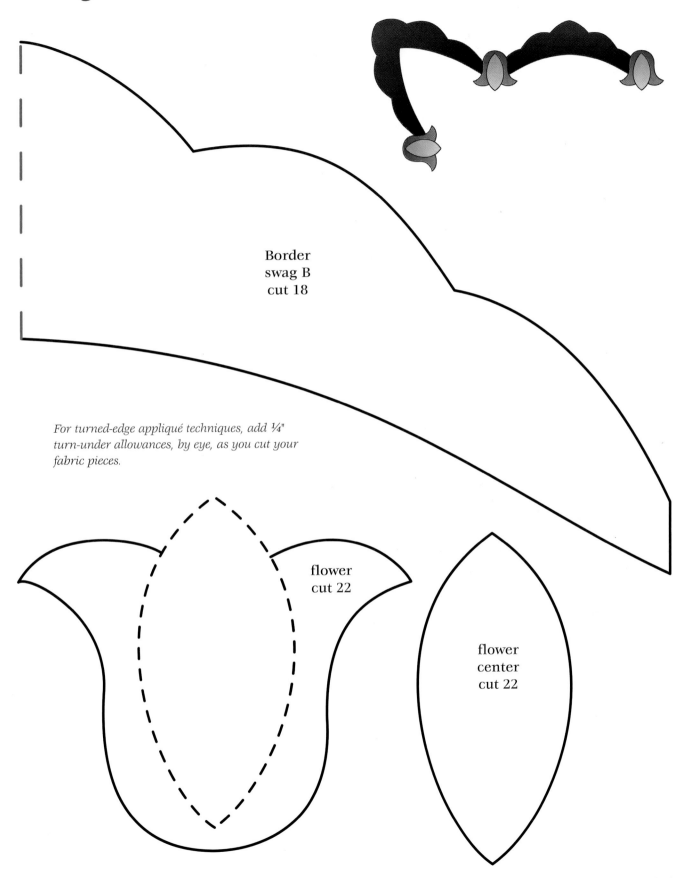

Border
swag B
cut 18

*For turned-edge appliqué techniques, add ¼"
turn-under allowances, by eye, as you cut your
fabric pieces.*

flower
cut 22

flower
center
cut 22

CHRISTMAS CHEER, 84" x 98". Bed quilt, pieced by the author and machine quilted by Quilt and Stitch Shop, Slayton, Oregon.

flower petal
cut 5

leaf
cut 4
& 4R

embroider
leaf veins

leaf
cut 4 & 4R

berry
cut 4

Easy Floral Appliqué Patterns ~ *Eula Mae Long*

Christmas Block CHRISTMAS CHEER

placement diagram
Full-sized patterns, on pages 76–77, for 14" block

Grid squares represent 3". Appliqué the
flowers in the order in which real flowers
grow: leaves then flowers.

*For turned-edge appliqué techniques,
add ¼" turn-under allowances, by eye,
as you cut your fabric pieces.*

petal pattern on page 76
make 1 flower

flower
center
cut 1

leaf
cut 8

Photo of VICTORIAN ROSE quilt shown
on page 3, the Dedication page

flower 2
cut 1

flower 2
center
cut 1

flower 2
center
cut 4

*For turned-edge appliqué techniques,
add ¼" turn-under allowances, by eye,
as you cut your fabric pieces.*

flower 2
cut 4

placement diagram
Full-sized patterns this page.

Grid squares represent 3".
Appliqué the flowers in the
order in which real flowers
grow: leaves then flowers.

About the Author

"It seems like I was born with a needle in my hand," says Eula Mae Long. She loved sewing so much that, in high school, she took four years of it in home economics. Then, while her children were in school, she took every sewing class the adult education system gave, including a nine-month power sewing class.

Next came a clothing color and design class at a junior college, which proved helpful for choosing colors when she began quilting. She first tried her hand at quilting when her grandchild was born. Eula Mae says, "The stitches in that Sunbonnet Sue and Overall Bill quilt had what we call 'toe catcher' stitches, but it lasted until grandson Chuck was about 10 years old."

On a cruise with Doreen Speckman, she discovered appliqué in a class taught by Nancy Pearson. Eula Mae has been quilting and taking quilt classes ever since. Along the way, she began teaching quilting with her good friend, Irma Woody. Then she discovered that she loved making her own appliqué designs. Others enjoyed her designs and encouraged her to share them with quilters, hence the publication of this book.

Other AQS Books

This is only a small selection of the books available from the American Quilter's Society. AQS books are known worldwide for timely topics, clear writing, beautiful color photos, and accurate illustrations and patterns. The following books are available from your local bookseller, quilt shop, or public library:

#6418   us$18.95

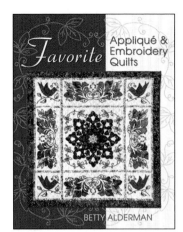

#6410   us$19.95

#6301   us$18.95

#6205   us$24.95

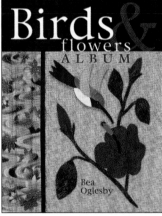

#6211   us$19.95

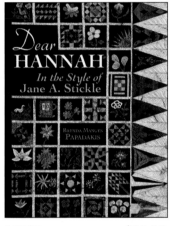

#6296   us$25.95

#5855   us$22.95

#6001   us$21.95

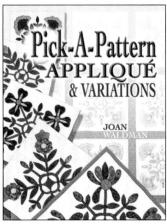

#6077   us$24.95

LOOK for these books nationally. CALL or VISIT our Web site at www.AQSquilt.com.

1-800-626-5420

Easy Floral Appliqué Patterns
by Eula Mae Long

LARGE BASKET, 31" x 35". Made by the author.